maybe later
I0759838
maybe later

This

No-Pressure Book Journal

belongs to

The No-Pressure Book Journal

A No-Guilt, No-Shame, No-Stress Journal to Help You Read Better and Enjoy Books Again

MALLORY O'MEARA & BREA GRANT

weldonowen

Contents

5 Introduction

10 Journal: What Kind of Reader Are You?

17 Essay: How to Get Out of a Book Slump

20 Journal: Your Reader Wheelhouse

23 Essay: Where to Get Book Recommendations

26 Journal: Your Reader Doghouse

29 Essay: Dump! That! Book!

32 Journal: Your Reading Doorways

35 Essay: Goals for the Reader You Are

38 Journal: Your Favorite Genres

41 Essay: Getting More Reading Done

44 Journal: Your TBR

55 Essay: How to Get Books

59 Tracking Your Reading

200 Additional Notes

221 Glossary

Introduction

Hello from your book pals, Brea and Mallory! Maybe you know who we are because you listen to our podcast, *Reading Glasses*, or maybe you picked this up because you liked the idea of a book journal that wasn't going to feel like work. (Or maybe you have no idea why you picked this up except that the universe compelled you to and that's okay too!) No matter what the reason, we're here to guide you to a better reading life.

We started our show in 2017 because we like talking about reading and solving the very specific problems of readers. How do you stop reading a book you don't like? How do you find more time to read? Where do you hide the bodies of all the people who keep interrupting your reading?

But, who are we?

Brea is a filmmaker and eReader extraordinaire who:

- stays up late trying to get just one more chapter in
- organizes her books by color
- loves to snack while reading
- uses anything nearby as a bookmark
- checks out loads of books from the library

Mallory is an author and book hoarder who:

- loves to inhale a novel in one sitting
- prefers print
- organizes her books by genre
- has a collection of laminated bookmarks
- buys way too many books

As you can see, we've got the whole spectrum of reading quirks covered. After years of helping bookworms, we wanted to put some of this bookish wisdom into, well, a book. This journal is for all kinds of readers—whether you read one book a year or one hundred, no matter what you read, or how you read it.

You picked this up, so you probably want to read, but let's say you need a little encouragement outside of avoiding people at a social gathering or escaping the horrors of everyday life.

Turns out, reading is good for you (who knew)! If you need a reason to pick up a book, here are a few:

READING MAKES YOU SMARTER. Reading novels can increase your intelligence! It ups your vocabulary, promotes critical thinking, and increases your memorization skills (yes, remembering all those characters in an epic fantasy novel does translate to your real life). Magnetic resonance imaging (MRI) has shown that people who read have increased activity in their brains. And, of course, nonfiction makes you smarter by giving you new information on subjects you're interested in and lots of facts to share at parties!

READING MAKES YOU MORE EMPATHETIC. We love this reason in a world that often feels like it is lacking empathy. When you read stories about someone else, you identify with their thoughts, feelings, and emotions and therefore become more empathetic to those around you.

READING CAN RELIEVE STRESS. Taking a break from the pressures of the world is a great way to relax. We will do anything to keep us from remembering that there is laundry that needs to be done! As little as six minutes of reading has been shown to reduce heart rate and muscle tension.

READING CAN HELP YOU SLEEP. Phones are somehow invading our sleeping patterns and will likely be the death of us all, but reading is the opposite. Reading before bed actually promotes good sleep!

READING CAN BE GOOD FOR YOUR MIND AS YOU AGE. Studies have shown that reading can slow mental decline and reduce the risk of Alzheimer's.

READING CAN HELP YOU LEARN TO FOCUS. We all know that it's hard to focus when you have a phone right at your fingertips that can order burgers, a karaoke machine, and that random shirt that was advertised to you. Reading can quiet some of that chatter and help you learn to focus.

READING IS FUN. This is our favorite one.

We've found that lots of people waste time reading books that *aren't right for them*. Most of us spent years being told what to read in school and never got to know who we really are as readers. It's time to change that!

Here are some scenarios we've heard in the past that may ring true for you:

- You didn't enjoy your English classes in high school (probably because they were serving up some stale classic literature that may not have been right for you) so you think you aren't a serious reader.

- You went to grad school, had a baby, or had a huge life change, which has given you less time to think about what you enjoy and now can't find anything that you can stick with.
- You used to love a particular type of book (long fantasy series, scary horror, celebrity memoirs, etc.) but now those books aren't hitting like they used to.
- You pick up books you've heard about but you never actually finish them.

If this sounds like you (and even if it doesn't!), *we can help*. We'll help you track your reading and, most importantly, learn more about yourself as you go. If you haven't really examined yourself as a reader, you may not know what you should be reading. If there's one thing we can guarantee, *there is a book out there for you*. (In fact, there are many!)

We'll get you back to reading and finding books you love without pressure, guilt, or shame. This journal will help you read better!

JOURNAL

What Kind of Reader Are You?

All right, let's start with where you are right now. Circle your answers below.

Do you feel pressure to read more?

Yes

No

How do you feel about reading challenges or goals?

They motivate me

They put too much pressure on me

Do you feel like you have a reading community (online counts!)?

Yes

No

Do you like to read in short or long sessions?

Short

Long

How about your to-be-read (TBR) list? Is it long or short?

It's overflowing

I have no idea what I'll read next

Do you often pick up a book and never finish it?

Yes

No

How do you feel about book recommendations?

I am overwhelmed by book suggestions from friends, family, social media, or podcasts

I want more suggestions

Do you finish books you don't like?

Yes

No

Check any of these that sound like something you'd like to read. None is okay too!

- ☐ **LITERARY FICTION**—A broad category of realistic fiction with a range of character developments.
- ☐ **MYSTERY**—Who did the crime? Who did the murdering?
- ☐ **THRILLER**—More tension than mystery with a focus on the crime unfolding.
- ☐ **CELEBRITY MEMOIRS**—Your favorite celebrity tells all . . . or at least some.
- ☐ **BIOGRAPHY**—A life story, told by someone else.
- ☐ **ROMANCE**—A story where the romance between two (or more!) characters is center stage.
- ☐ **YA**—Young adults are the protagonists! It can be fiction, horror, fantasy, or any other genre.
- ☐ **FANTASY**—A fantastical world with magical and mythical creatures.
- ☐ **SCIENCE FICTION**—A futuristic world with imagined technologies, people, and environments.
- ☐ **HORROR**—A story meant to scare you in any genre! From your average spooky tale to poop-your-pants scares.
- ☐ **NONFICTION**—History, science, and any other category that focuses on facts, real people, and real events.
- ☐ **MICROHISTORY**—A history of a very specific thing, like . . . forks.

There are lots more genres and many of these are crossovers—romantasy (romance fantasy), literary thrillers (probably becoming a movie as we write this), and YA horror, just to name a few!

Answer the following questions about your reading experience.

How many books did you read last year? Was it more or less than the year before?

Have you gone through a change in your reading habits recently?

Where do you hear about new books?

What was the last book you really loved reading?

Based on all of the above, what do you want to change or improve about your reading life?

Take a look at the last three books you loved. Write down what you liked about them—the more specific, the better. Did they take place on a beach and you loved that? Did one of the characters have a cool job? Was it written in emails back and forth between the characters (that's called epistolary!)?

Okay. Now, really think about the answers of this section critically. If you don't like book suggestions, why are you on BookTok all day? If you are only interested in nonfiction, why are you picking up the latest in Oprah's Book Club? We want you to really think about who you are before you force yourself to read something that someone said you should.

maybe
later

ESSAY

How to Get Out of a Book Slump

Ah, yes. The dreaded *book slump*. You never see it coming. You pick up a book and you get halfway through and put it aside. Then . . . you do it again. Then you look at your TBR list and realize you don't want to read *any* of the books on there. What the heck is happening?!

If you are tired of reading, not excited about your current book, or your mind is wandering every time you try to read even a page, you may be in a book slump.

We define a *book slump* as a time in which you are no longer excited or motivated by reading. It can be for weeks, months, or even years at a time. Don't blame yourself! It happens to everyone. Also, *don't blame reading*. We see that all too often! People hit a wall, not enjoying a few books in a row, and they give up on books altogether!

First, make sure this is a reading-based issue. We are not therapists and if your slump includes not being able to concentrate all day, not being able to get out of bed, or not finding joy in life, then please seek professional help from an amazing therapist. Not us. We are podcasters only.

Here are our slump-busting tips:

IDENTIFY IT. If you think you are in a slump, you probably are. If looking at your current read is giving you a dreadful, overwhelmed, or unhappy feeling, then you are in a slump! And it's time to get out of it!

DUMP YOUR BOOK. Stop the book you're reading immediately. Don't worry—books rarely disappear from Earth and you can return to it another time.

FIND SOMETHING EASIER. No honkers (very long books), no dense academic nonfiction, no thousand-page sci-fi books. Find something you can get through easily. A lighter book. A novella. A graphic novel. Get out of the genre you read all the time or try something that is a little easier on your brain. Once you actually get through a book, you're going to feel a lot better about reading and finishing something!

ABANDON YOUR READING GOALS. If you were trying to hit a reading goal this year, this is not the time. Trying to finish up a certain number of pages before the end of the year? Forget it! The only goal is to find something you actually enjoy reading.

PICK SOMETHING THAT FEELS LIKE A TREAT. For Brea, it's a graphic novel. For Mallory, it's a middle-grade horror book. Choose something that is the chocolate cake of reading, the book that you've been saving because it looks so good.

MAKE THE EXPERIENCE FUN AND RELAXING. Is it next to a pool in the sun? Is it snuggled up on the couch with your favorite candle lit and a mug of cocoa? Is it listening to a book while on a long hike? Whatever it is, think about the experience of reading and not just the book itself.

Try all of these until you find a book that you look forward to reading. Reading should be fun. It's good for you. But it shouldn't feel like eating your vegetables (unless you like vegetables and then yes, it feels like that).

JOURNAL

Your Reader Wheelhouse

We define a *reader wheelhouse* as something that makes you want to pick up a book. Knowing this information can help you easily pick your next favorite read! It can include but isn't limited to the following:

Subjects, tropes, genres and subgenres, types of protagonist, specific settings, particular authors, writing styles

Some popular *Reading Glasses* listener wheelhouse items are retellings, multiple storylines, time travel, enemies to lovers, LGBTQIA+ protagonists, and strong female characters. Brea's includes sci-fi, books set in space, illustrated poetry collections, and magical food. Mallory's includes haunted houses, werewolves, books set in Florida, and weird fiction. Write your reader wheelhouse below!

HOT BOOK TIP

Hey, it's Brea! I like to revisit my wheelhouse every once in a while. As readers (and people), we're always changing and so are our tastes. If you notice you've recently loved multiple books with the same theme or subject (dark academia, rom-coms, or characters in the gray moral area, for example), then consider putting it in your wheelhouse!

ESSAY

Where to Get Book Recommendations

So now you know which books to look for. But the question is, *Where do you find recommendations?*

Obviously, we've got loads of recommendations on *Reading Glasses* (out every Thursday with hundreds of back episodes for your listening pleasure), but there are many places to find great book suggestions.

PODCASTS—There are many fantastic podcasts that recommend books every week. Not every host is going to have the same taste as you, so look for one that recommends books you like. Brea gets a lot of recommendations from other bookish podcasts!

AN AUTHOR YOU LOVE—You just read a book you loved. We say . . . keep going! Try a backlist book by that author. Also, see what this author has reviewed and what they are talking about on their social media. If you like the books they write, you'll probably like the books they read! Mallory looks for blurbs on a book jacket from authors she loves.

WEBSITES AND BLOGS—We could list these all day, but by the time this book goes to print, it will be dated because the internet moves fast, y'all. So, we suggest doing a specific search for what you want—"space pirates," "morally gray characters," "novels with short chapters"—and see what comes up. There are tons of websites that make wonderful book lists!

YOUR LOCAL LIBRARIAN OR BOOKSELLER—We love librarians and booksellers! They are here to help you in many ways, but one of their favorites is recommending books. These folks are around books all day and can definitely tell you what is hot and happening, or cater a recommendation directly to your tastes.

YOUR FRIENDS AND FAMILY—Try asking, "What are you reading?" or "What's something great you've read lately?" At the very least, you are going to end up in a great conversation and probably learn something new about someone you like. At the very best, you'll get a great book!

With the explosion of BookTok, Bookstagram, and other social media sites, it's easy to be overwhelmed by recommendations. (Seriously, how do people have time to read all those books?) But just because someone is saying they would *die for this book it's amazing you have to read it,* it may not be right for you. How will you know? Well, you just figured out your wheelhouse and if this book has no crossover with that wheelhouse, then it may not be for you. Also, once you find a trusted source, you will want to come back to them again and again.

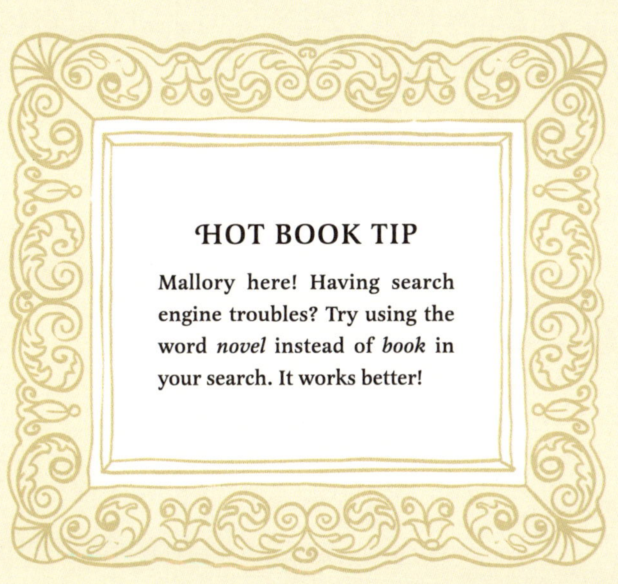

HOT BOOK TIP

Mallory here! Having search engine troubles? Try using the word *novel* instead of *book* in your search. It works better!

JOURNAL

Your Reader Doghouse

You worked on your wheelhouse, so now it's time to figure out your doghouse! We use the term *doghouse* to mean *any subjects, tropes, authors, genres, or writing styles that make you want to dump a book*.

It's important to know this so you can avoid reading things you don't like. There are so many books out there that you *will* like. Why waste your time with ones you won't? That's like dating someone for years who you can't stand. And while this isn't a dating advice book, we suggest not doing that either.

Think of the last few books you put down or forced your way through. Was there something in them that made you not want to finish them? Something that put you off or made you uncomfortable? Did the characters bore you? Some examples from the Glasser community: *love triangles, animal death, suicide, bad writing, switching between first and third person in the writing*. Brea's doghouse includes holier-than-thou self-help books, judgmental characters, and complicated writing. Mallory's includes snakes, love triangles, and sexual assault.

HOT BOOK TIP

Hey, it's Mallory again. Your doghouse can be fluid! Maybe you just don't want to read about a certain thing *right now*, but you'll be okay with it in the future. When you're not enjoying a book, try to pinpoint why it isn't clicking with you. (And stop reading it!) Then, come back to this list, and maybe add something new (or take something off). One day, I might be able to read about love triangles again. Or they'll always make me want to pull my hair out. Protagonist, you need to pick one!

ESSAY

Dump! That! Book!

We've all had it happen.

You start reading a book, maybe one you've really been anticipating. You crack it open, smell that sweet scent of a new book (no? just us?), and soon, to your despair, you realize that you just don't like it. The protagonist is annoying. The plot is boring. The writing style is difficult to follow.

And yet, you keep reading.

The further you get, the worse you feel, and somehow, the less you're able to give up. You can barely bring yourself to pick the book up, yet you can't quit. You're trapped. You don't want to read this book anymore, but you feel guilty throwing in the towel. Why? This is something we like to call the *sunken page fallacy*.

The sunken cost fallacy is a phenomenon where you find yourself reluctant to abandon something because you have invested heavily in it, with time or money perhaps, even when it is quite clear that the abandonment is the most beneficial thing for you to do. It's like that one piece of clothing you have in your closet that you never wear, yet refuse to donate, because you spent too much money on it.

When this happens to readers, it's the sunken *page* fallacy. You feel too guilty to dump the book because of the hours you already spent reading it, or because of the money you spent on it, or because someone you love gave it to you. No matter how many times you tell Aunt Donna that it's weird for her to buy you gargoyle erotica, now you're stuck with an entire series full of stone . . . well, you know.

The sunken page fallacy is one of the top causes for book slumps. Reading a book you don't like is almost guaranteed to make reading feel like a chore. So, we're here to tell you: Dump! that! book!

If you're not enjoying a book, stop reading.

We'll even give you permission if you need it. That book you haven't touched in a month? Dump it. That novel you've been halfway through all year? Dump it. That thriller you keep hoping will get good? *Dump it*. (Do you want a signed permission slip? Email us.)

Maybe it's not that the book is bad. Maybe it's just not the right time for you to read it. So much of our reading experience is what we bring to the book, and maybe right now, your brain is just not a good match for this particular title. Remember, you can always pick it back up again someday. The book won't burst into flames if you stick it back on the shelf. This is not your only chance to read it.

There are so many good books in the world! You're going to die someday without having read all the books you want to read. Don't waste your time with a dud! Imagine being on your deathbed and regretting all the hours you lost to that weird book your coworker wanted you to read.

If you are reading for enjoyment or personal betterment, slogging your way through a book you hate is not going to help. Pick up a book that excites you, that compels you to keep reading it, that you think about when you're at work. Your new favorite book is calling your name, but you can't hear it because you are trying to finish the book your ex gave you for Christmas five years ago.

HOT BOOK TIP

Brea here. How do you know when to dump a book? It's up to you. You'll probably know! Mallory usually knows after one chapter. I like to give it around 10 percent. Sometimes, I dump a book within one or two pages . . . or with only a few chapters to go! That's right. Even when you've already read two hundred pages, if you're feeling bored, you can dump it.

Ask yourself: Are you engaged with the story? Are you curious about what's going to happen? Are you having fun? If the answer is no, you know what you have to do. We release you! Right now, we are relieving you of that book guilt. You're free.

JOURNAL

Your Reading Doorways

Developed by librarian Nancy Pearl, the concept of a reading doorway means the element of the book that makes you fall in love with it. Either *plot, character, setting*, or *language*. Everyone has one or two that they feel strongly about. Whether you're a language person and you look for lyrical writing, or you're extremely plot driven, or you are drawn to an interesting setting, or you care about the character most of all, one of these four doorways fits you.

Knowing your doorway, like knowing your reader wheelhouse, will help you find more five-star reads. If you have an understanding of why you love the books you love, then you can find more books like them! Recommend someone a book, and they'll read for a week. Teach someone to figure out their reading doorway, and they'll find books for life.

Brea is a setting-first reader. Is it in space? On a creepy, postapocalyptic road? Is there a lot of sand for some reason? She's all in. Mallory is a plot-first reader. She wants the first page to suck her in and make her desperate to know what happened.

Now, how do you figure out which one you are? Ask yourself these questions: When recommending a book, which doorway do you always mention? Which doorway makes you want to pick up a book? Which doorway keeps you hooked on a story? Look at the last few books you've loved. Which doorway stands out for each?

Rank your reading doorways below.

1. ______________________________

2. ______________________________

3. ______________________________

4. ______________________________

ESSAY

Goals for the Reader You Are

If there are things you want to change about your reading life, it can be helpful to set goals. Maybe you want to read more books every year, or get through your TBR pile, or there's a reading challenge you want to complete.

The key is choosing goals for the reader you are, or the reader you can be. Depending on what type of person you are, goals might make reading more exciting, or turn it into a fraught chore.

Before you even begin to choose reader goals, you need to ask yourself: Do goals motivate you? Or do they stress you out? Will you find yourself satisfied with whatever progress you made at the end of a month, or will you find yourself crying, trying to hold a book with each limb and read them all simultaneously?

Brea and Mallory both ride the line in between. We each enjoy having goals to give us some extra motivation, but can get stressed out if we fall behind. Mallory especially can be, if she's not careful, prone to panic reading like she's back in high school English class the night before a big test.

If reading goals motivate you, just make sure to look at your current reading life before setting them. If you read twenty books a year, maybe bumping it up to one hundred is too big of a jump. You don't want to find yourself faced with a three-hundred-hour readathon at the end of December. Set a goal within a reasonable range of what you do now. You can always increase the number next month, or next year!

If reading goals stress you out, why are you setting them? We're serious! Ultimately, reading is supposed to be fun. It's not homework, it's not a chore. We know it's tough after years of assigned reading in school to train your brain to think of books as an exclusively fun activity. With any hobby that features progress, or that feels productive, it can be difficult not to feel like you're behind. But at the risk of sounding like someone who works at a cheesy theme park, you can't be behind on fun! The point is to enjoy reading, not to simply *have read*.

Plus, you're probably reading more than you think you are. According to a study published in the *Washington Post* in 2024, 46 percent of Americans don't read at all. So, if you're reading a single book a year, you're already reading more than almost half the country. Of readers, the top 33 percent read five books a year, the top 21 percent read ten books a year, and only the tippity top, the 1 percent, read more than fifty. Take this into consideration when you're setting your yearly goals. Statistically, you're probably already reading a lot!

Remember, you are in control of your reading life. Goals are not the boss of you. Regularly check in with your objectives. Are you making steady progress? Are you feeling guilty if you aren't? Are you enjoying yourself?

If it's been a few months, and you haven't even started on all those poetry books you wanted to read, or you haven't hit your weekly target page count once, it's probably time to adjust. Or throw the whole goal in the trash! *You haven't failed.* A good goal is one that is attainable to you, *even if it seems like it should be easy*. If it's not attainable and it's making you feel terrible, it's just a bad goal. You're not a bad reader.

So, take a look at your reading life. What would you like to change? Is there a type of book you always wanted to try, or read more of? Do you want to try to finish a book every week? Do you have any social-justice goals, like reading more BIPOC authors, or more books with LGBTQIA+ protagonists? There are all sorts of ways to improve your reading life.

Whatever the goal is, make sure achieving it will result in a happier you, not just a more productive you. Choose something that makes you excited to work on it, something that you feel will genuinely make your reading life better. We believe in you!

HOT BOOK TIP

Hey, it's Mallory. If you are easily stressed out by feeling beholden to goals, but still want to make changes to your reading life, look at what you can do without having to set a numerical goal! Brea recently had a goal of reading more backlist books from her TBR list instead of constantly picking up new releases. Not only was she successful, but it made her feel great and on top of her gigantic TBR. I personally enjoyed hitting a goal of reading in public more. I made a point to take my current book with me to parks, bars, and coffee shops. It was so fun!

JOURNAL

Your Favorite Genres

Genres are essentially labels to help an author or a publisher get a book in the hands of the right audience. What's your favorite book genre? Maybe you love broad categories, like literary fiction or science fiction. Or maybe you like to get into specifics, like cozy romantasy or isolated space horror. Brea is the sci-fi queen, while Mallory cannot resist the call of a horror book.

Look at the most recent books you've really loved, and check what genre they are. List them below. If you can, try to note the details. What time period does it take place in? What age group is it aimed at? What tone does it have: terrifying, happy, bleak? Knowing what genres you really enjoy is another tool to help you find more books you'll love.

TITLE: ____________________

GENRE: ____________________

TIME PERIOD: ____________________

AGE GROUP: ____________________

TONE: ____________________

TITLE: ____________________

GENRE: ____________________

TIME PERIOD: ____________________

AGE GROUP: ____________________

TONE: ____________________

TITLE: ___

GENRE: ___

TIME PERIOD: ___

AGE GROUP: ___

TONE: ___

TITLE: ___

GENRE: ___

TIME PERIOD: ___

AGE GROUP: ___

TONE: ___

TITLE: ___

GENRE: ___

TIME PERIOD: ___

AGE GROUP: ___

TONE: ___

HOT BOOK TIP

Brea again! Is there a genre you've always been curious about, but you're not sure where to start? Try finding a book in that genre that was popular within the past few years, but isn't overwhelmingly buzzy right now. Awards lists from past years are a great place to look!

ESSAY

Getting More Reading Done

It's the holy grail for book lovers. It's what everyone yearns for, but rarely gets to have.

More time to read.

In a perfect world, no one would have to run errands, do chores, or answer emails. We could read all we wanted, inhaling whole series at a time. Sadly, most of us are stuck carving out reading time when we can, fitting it in between all the zillion things we have to get done every day to stay alive, and clean, and pay our bills.

No matter how much you wish for it, you're not going to be magically granted an extra hour every day to read. We all want more reading time, and the way to get it is to make it ourselves. If you want to read more, you have to prioritize it. Time to roll up your sleeves.

Take a realistic look at your daily or weekly schedule. Where in your day could you fit some reading in? What do you do on your lunch break? How much time, really, are you spending on social media? Do you have a spare half hour before you get out of bed, or before you fall asleep at night? Brea reads every night before bed, even if it means she falls asleep with her face in her Kindle.

If adding *read* to your daily to-do list won't stress you out, this is something we highly recommend. Brea and Mallory both do this. We love checking something off a list. It's a reminder to take time for yourself every day and do something that makes you happy. Also, if you are a to-do list fiend like we are, sometimes the sheer joy of crossing something off that list is enough to motivate you.

Do you have the physical ability to try other book formats? Trying e-books or audiobooks can make reading possible in new areas of your life. Audiobooks while driving, e-books on your phone while you're waiting in line at the post office? Branching out with formats can hugely increase the amount of reading time in your day. Brea listens to audiobooks while she walks her dog. Mallory loves listening to them when she's folding laundry and cleaning the house. It helps her reach her reading goals *and* makes scrubbing the toilet somewhat fun. Or at least slightly tolerable.

But what about when you actually do have reading time, and you can't focus?

It finally happened. You have an hour to yourself. No laundry to fold, no meetings to attend, nothing but you, your book, and maybe some snacks. You sit down and, instead of devouring your book, you can't stop looking at your phone. Suddenly, the whole hour has flown by, and all you've managed to do is get through one single page and buy something off Instagram.

First, be nice to yourself. Maybe you needed to zone out for an hour. Maybe that shirt you bought on Instagram will look nice. The moment you start self-flagellating about reading is the moment it stops being fun.

Second, try to funnel your focus toward your book. Leave your phone in another room for a while. Put on some background music or ambient noise (maybe even something that goes well with the genre of your book!). Set a timer and try to read until it goes off.

Keeping up a reading schedule in the face of all the distractions we have is about consistency. Try to make reading a habit. If you can't always read at the same time, try to at least read every day. Even just one chapter, even just one *page* a day will get you on the way to finishing a book. Pages really add up—reading just a single chapter a day means you could finish the average book in a month. Reading every day, even just a little, will also keep your brain in reading shape. The more you read, the more you are *used* to reading, which means the more you'll be able to quickly focus and stay engaged with your book. And of course, reading a great book that you're dying to finish always helps.

Prioritize reading, make it a habit, and be nice to yourself when you can't. There's no minimum daily page count required to call yourself a reader. Get that book out and enjoy yourself!

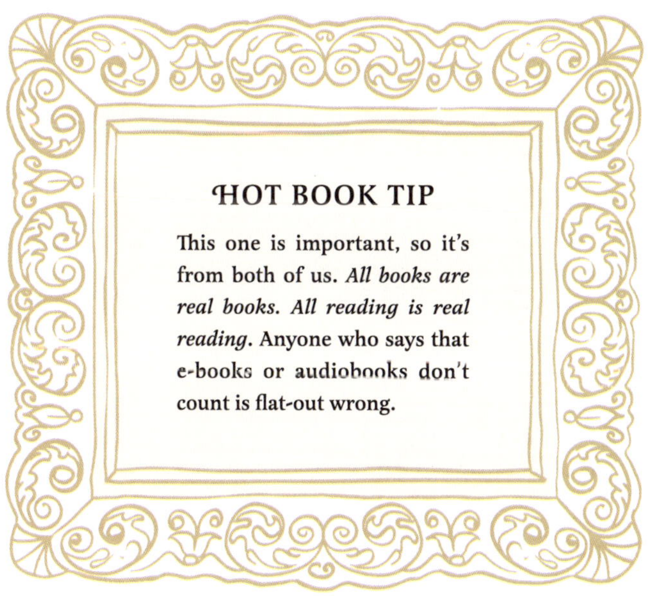

HOT BOOK TIP

This one is important, so it's from both of us. *All books are real books. All reading is real reading*. Anyone who says that e-books or audiobooks don't count is flat-out wrong.

JOURNAL

Your TBR

TBR is one of the most used terms in the reader world. It stands for to be read, and it's usually in reference to the CVS-receipt-sized list of books you'd like to read. It can be an actual list in a notebook, a spreadsheet on your phone, a physical pile of books by your bedside, or just a free-floating group of books in your head. Whatever form your TBR takes, it's a good idea to keep one so that when you finish a book, you've got titles to choose from for your next read.

Just like your reader goals, make sure that your TBR looks exciting, not overwhelming. A TBR list should be like a refrigerator full of tasty snacks to eat, not a pile of homework. If having an infinite list is fun for you, go for it! But you might need to regularly trim yours if going above a certain number—five, ten, one hundred, five hundred—stresses you out. Brea, for example, keeps a gigantic list in her phone. Mallory, on the other hand, gets too overwhelmed and keeps a physical shelf that can't go over ten books.

What to put on your list? Any book that sounds like something you'd want to read!

HOT BOOK TIP

Brea here! You can use the note section to remind yourself of why the book sounded good in the first place, such as "spooky house, lesbian protagonist, historical" or "talking dog, spaceship, funny" (which sounds like a book I want to read!), or where you got the recommendation from, such as a friend, or a book podcast.

Use the following pages for your TBR. You can also tape a piece of paper or put a sticky note onto it to either add to or change your list.

TITLE: ____________________

AUTHOR: ____________________

NOTE: ____________________

____

____

TITLE: ____________________

AUTHOR: ____________________

NOTE: ____________________

____

____

TITLE: ____________________

AUTHOR: ____________________

NOTE: ____________________

____

____

My TBR

TITLE: ______________________

AUTHOR: ______________________

NOTE: ______________________

____

TITLE: ______________________

AUTHOR: ______________________

NOTE: ______________________

____

TITLE: ______________________

AUTHOR: ______________________

NOTE: ______________________

____

TITLE: ______________________

AUTHOR: ______________________

NOTE: ______________________

____

TITLE: ______________________

AUTHOR: ______________________

NOTE: ______________________

____

My TBR

TITLE: ______________________________

AUTHOR: ______________________________

NOTE: ______________________________

____

TITLE: ______________________________

AUTHOR: ______________________________

NOTE: ______________________________

____

TITLE: ______________________________

AUTHOR: ______________________________

NOTE: ______________________________

____

TITLE: ______________________________

AUTHOR: ______________________________

NOTE: ______________________________

____

TITLE: ______________________________

AUTHOR: ______________________________

NOTE: ______________________________

____

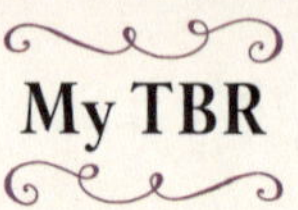

My TBR

TITLE: ____________________

AUTHOR: ____________________

NOTE: ____________________

TITLE: ____________________

AUTHOR: ____________________

NOTE: ____________________

TITLE: ____________________

AUTHOR: ____________________

NOTE: ____________________

TITLE: ____________________

AUTHOR: ____________________

NOTE: ____________________

TITLE: ____________________

AUTHOR: ____________________

NOTE: ____________________

My TBR

TITLE:

AUTHOR:

NOTE:

TITLE:

AUTHOR:

NOTE:

TITLE:

AUTHOR:

NOTE:

TITLE:

AUTHOR:

NOTE:

TITLE:

AUTHOR:

NOTE:

My TBR

TITLE: ___

AUTHOR: ___

NOTE: ___

___

TITLE: ___

AUTHOR: ___

NOTE: ___

___

TITLE: ___

AUTHOR: ___

NOTE: ___

___

TITLE: ___

AUTHOR: ___

NOTE: ___

___

TITLE: ___

AUTHOR: ___

NOTE: ___

___

My TBR

TITLE:

AUTHOR:

NOTE:

TITLE:

AUTHOR:

NOTE:

TITLE:

AUTHOR:

NOTE:

TITLE:

AUTHOR:

NOTE:

TITLE:

AUTHOR:

NOTE:

My TBR

TITLE: ______

AUTHOR: ______

NOTE: ______

______

TITLE: ______

AUTHOR: ______

NOTE: ______

______

TITLE: ______

AUTHOR: ______

NOTE: ______

______

TITLE: ______

AUTHOR: ______

NOTE: ______

______

TITLE: ______

AUTHOR: ______

NOTE: ______

______

My TBR

TITLE: ______

AUTHOR: ______

NOTE: ______

______

TITLE: ______

AUTHOR: ______

NOTE: ______

______

TITLE: ______

AUTHOR: ______

NOTE: ______

______

TITLE: ______

AUTHOR: ______

NOTE: ______

______

TITLE: ______

AUTHOR: ______

NOTE: ______

______

ESSAY

How to Get Books

Okay, we've given you all our hottest tips on reading and you're all ready to get some books.

But where do you go?

There's a lot of discourse in the bookish world about the best places to get books from, both in person and online. What is the most ethical? What benefits authors the most? Where do you get the best value? We know that trying to be a good bookish citizen can be difficult. How do you balance these questions with convenience and budgets?

The answer is that you do your best.

You can never, ever go wrong with buying books at an independent bookstore. If you don't have one locally, most indies have online stores that you can browse and will ship your purchases to you. Even though indie bookstores can't sell books at the discounted prices like some websites can, they're the ones putting on author events, handselling books they love, offering specific recommendations for you, and generally being pillars of the bookish community. Plus, many sell signed editions!

We understand that the internet is convenient. Everyone buys things online! Of course, some online places are better to buy books from than others, both for the book world *and* for you. For example, Barnes & Noble often has very cool special editions of books to preorder. And many indie bookstores have Bookshop.org affiliate links so that when you order, a percentage of your purchase goes back to them.

You also don't have to spend money at all! You might not realize it, but every time you check out a book—whether that's a print book, an audiobook, or an e-book—from the library, you're helping the author that wrote it *and* the library that carries it. Libraries buy books, and the more a book gets checked out, the more a library is likely to buy another copy of it. Higher book circulation numbers help libraries when they're applying for their budget. Authors love when you get their books at the library, librarians love when you get books at the library, and you should love getting books at the library because they're free!

People ask us all the time, as both authors and book podcasters, where they should get a book from that will benefit an author the most. The answer is a library or any bookstore that is selling a new copy of the book. Getting a used copy, an advance review copy, or a pirated copy does not benefit the author at all. We do love a used bookstore, and getting books from one benefits the store, many of which serve as bookish community hubs. But if you want an author to get paid for the work they did, you've got to buy a new copy or check it out from the library.

What about buying e-books and audiobooks? There are a lot of options out there. Some, like Libro.fm, are independent companies. Some are corporate giants that probably don't need your money and won't be reinvesting that back into the community. But we get it, they're so easy to order from!

Ultimately, the best place to get books from is a store or website that doesn't break your budget or cause you stress. Brea and Mallory have both settled into a system that combines their favorite ways to get books. We preorder books from authors that we already love, put books we're really interested in but not absolutely certain we'll like on hold at the library, and sometimes pick up older, backlist titles at used bookstores and library sales.

We try to put our money into independent bookstores and places that support the bookish community, and we'd love it if you tried to. But all you can do is your best!

Tracking Your Reading

All right, you're ready to read and start tracking books!

The purpose of tracking your reading is to help you remember what you read, and most importantly, what you thought of what you read. You can use this information to find more books you'll love, hit any reading goals you have, and learn more about yourself as a reader.

What should you track? Whatever you want! Really, whatever you think you're going to find useful. The title and the author are the bare minimum, but you can add your own review, any wheelhouse items, how long the book is, where you got the recommendation from, the format, how long it took you to read—the possibilities are truly endless. Track what you care about. Brea keeps it short and sweet with just the title and author. Mallory likes to include a letter grade for each book, along with a list of wheelhouse items.

When should you track? Some people immediately fill out their journal as soon as they're done with a book, some people wait a few days to digest the story, some people sit down once a month. Whatever works for you! As soon as Brea finishes a book, she adds it to her digital tracker. Mallory, on the other hand, sits down with her print book tracking journal every few weeks. There's no wrong way to track.

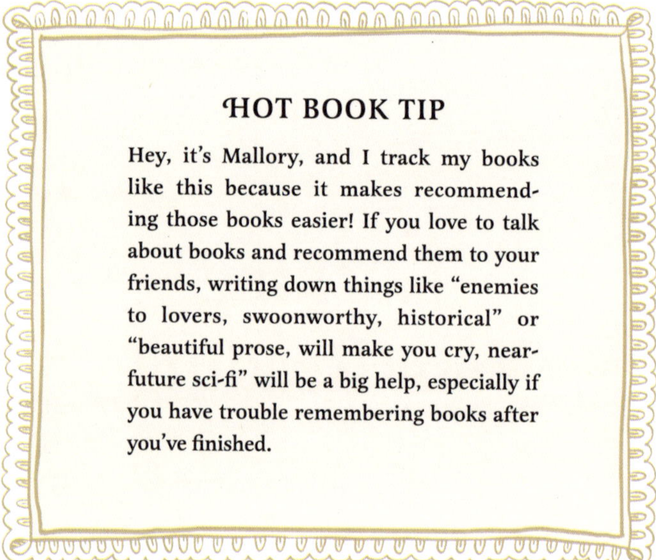

HOT BOOK TIP

Hey, it's Mallory, and I track my books like this because it makes recommending those books easier! If you love to talk about books and recommend them to your friends, writing down things like "enemies to lovers, swoonworthy, historical" or "beautiful prose, will make you cry, near-future sci-fi" will be a big help, especially if you have trouble remembering books after you've finished.

Just remember:

All books are real books, and all readers are real readers. Don't let any pressure, guilt, or shame clog up your reading life and get you into a book slump. And if you need any more help, we release our show every week with bookish advice.

Happy reading!

My Book Tracker

TITLE	AUTHOR
WHEELHOUSE	DOORWAY
THOUGHTS & QUOTES	
CONTENT WARNINGS	RATING

My Book Tracker

TITLE	AUTHOR
WHEELHOUSE	DOORWAY

THOUGHTS & QUOTES

CONTENT WARNINGS	RATING

My Book Tracker

TITLE	AUTHOR

WHEELHOUSE	DOORWAY

THOUGHTS & QUOTES

CONTENT WARNINGS	RATING

My Book Tracker

TITLE	AUTHOR
WHEELHOUSE	DOORWAY

THOUGHTS & QUOTES

CONTENT WARNINGS	RATING

My Book Tracker

TITLE	AUTHOR
WHEELHOUSE	DOORWAY

THOUGHTS & QUOTES

CONTENT WARNINGS	RATING

My Book Tracker

TITLE	AUTHOR
WHEELHOUSE	DOORWAY

THOUGHTS & QUOTES

CONTENT WARNINGS	RATING

My Book Tracker

TITLE	AUTHOR

WHEELHOUSE	DOORWAY

THOUGHTS & QUOTES

CONTENT WARNINGS	RATING

My Book Tracker

TITLE	AUTHOR
WHEELHOUSE	DOORWAY
THOUGHTS & QUOTES	
CONTENT WARNINGS	RATING

My Book Tracker

TITLE	AUTHOR
WHEELHOUSE	DOORWAY

THOUGHTS & QUOTES

CONTENT WARNINGS	RATING

My Book Tracker

TITLE	AUTHOR
WHEELHOUSE	DOORWAY

THOUGHTS & QUOTES

CONTENT WARNINGS	RATING

My Book Tracker

TITLE	AUTHOR
WHEELHOUSE	**DOORWAY**
THOUGHTS & QUOTES	
CONTENT WARNINGS	**RATING**

My Book Tracker

TITLE	**AUTHOR**
WHEELHOUSE	**DOORWAY**

THOUGHTS & QUOTES

CONTENT WARNINGS	**RATING**

My Book Tracker

TITLE

AUTHOR

WHEELHOUSE

DOORWAY

THOUGHTS & QUOTES

CONTENT WARNINGS

RATING

My Book Tracker

TITLE	AUTHOR
WHEELHOUSE	DOORWAY

THOUGHTS & QUOTES

CONTENT WARNINGS	RATING

My Book Tracker

TITLE	AUTHOR

WHEELHOUSE	DOORWAY

THOUGHTS & QUOTES

CONTENT WARNINGS	RATING

My Book Tracker

TITLE	AUTHOR

WHEELHOUSE	DOORWAY

THOUGHTS & QUOTES

CONTENT WARNINGS	RATING

My Book Tracker

TITLE	AUTHOR
WHEELHOUSE	**DOORWAY**

THOUGHTS & QUOTES

CONTENT WARNINGS	RATING

My Book Tracker

TITLE	AUTHOR

WHEELHOUSE	DOORWAY

THOUGHTS & QUOTES

CONTENT WARNINGS	RATING

My Book Tracker

TITLE	AUTHOR
WHEELHOUSE	**DOORWAY**
THOUGHTS & QUOTES	
CONTENT WARNINGS	**RATING**

My Book Tracker

TITLE	**AUTHOR**
WHEELHOUSE	**DOORWAY**

THOUGHTS & QUOTES

CONTENT WARNINGS	**RATING**

My Book Tracker

TITLE	**AUTHOR**
WHEELHOUSE	**DOORWAY**

THOUGHTS & QUOTES

CONTENT WARNINGS	**RATING**

My Book Tracker

TITLE	AUTHOR
WHEELHOUSE	DOORWAY

THOUGHTS & QUOTES

CONTENT WARNINGS	RATING

My Book Tracker

TITLE	AUTHOR

WHEELHOUSE	DOORWAY

THOUGHTS & QUOTES

CONTENT WARNINGS	RATING

My Book Tracker

TITLE	AUTHOR
WHEELHOUSE	**DOORWAY**

THOUGHTS & QUOTES

CONTENT WARNINGS	RATING

My Book Tracker

TITLE	AUTHOR
WHEELHOUSE	DOORWAY

THOUGHTS & QUOTES

CONTENT WARNINGS	RATING

My Book Tracker

TITLE	AUTHOR
WHEELHOUSE	DOORWAY

THOUGHTS & QUOTES

CONTENT WARNINGS	RATING

My Book Tracker

TITLE	AUTHOR
WHEELHOUSE	DOORWAY

THOUGHTS & QUOTES

CONTENT WARNINGS	RATING

My Book Tracker

TITLE	AUTHOR
WHEELHOUSE	DOORWAY

THOUGHTS & QUOTES

CONTENT WARNINGS	RATING

My Book Tracker

TITLE	AUTHOR
WHEELHOUSE	DOORWAY
THOUGHTS & QUOTES	
CONTENT WARNINGS	RATING

My Book Tracker

TITLE	AUTHOR
WHEELHOUSE	DOORWAY

THOUGHTS & QUOTES

CONTENT WARNINGS	RATING

My Book Tracker

TITLE	AUTHOR
WHEELHOUSE	DOORWAY
THOUGHTS & QUOTES	
CONTENT WARNINGS	RATING

My Book Tracker

TITLE	AUTHOR
WHEELHOUSE	DOORWAY

THOUGHTS & QUOTES

CONTENT WARNINGS	RATING

My Book Tracker

TITLE	AUTHOR
WHEELHOUSE	DOORWAY
THOUGHTS & QUOTES	
CONTENT WARNINGS	RATING

My Book Tracker

TITLE	AUTHOR
WHEELHOUSE	DOORWAY

THOUGHTS & QUOTES

CONTENT WARNINGS	RATING

My Book Tracker

TITLE	AUTHOR
WHEELHOUSE	**DOORWAY**

THOUGHTS & QUOTES

CONTENT WARNINGS	RATING

My Book Tracker

TITLE	AUTHOR

WHEELHOUSE	DOORWAY

THOUGHTS & QUOTES

CONTENT WARNINGS	RATING

My Book Tracker

TITLE	AUTHOR

WHEELHOUSE	DOORWAY

THOUGHTS & QUOTES

CONTENT WARNINGS	RATING

My Book Tracker

TITLE	AUTHOR
WHEELHOUSE	DOORWAY

THOUGHTS & QUOTES

CONTENT WARNINGS	RATING

My Book Tracker

TITLE	AUTHOR
WHEELHOUSE	DOORWAY

THOUGHTS & QUOTES

CONTENT WARNINGS	RATING

My Book Tracker

TITLE	AUTHOR
WHEELHOUSE	DOORWAY

THOUGHTS & QUOTES

CONTENT WARNINGS	RATING

My Book Tracker

TITLE	AUTHOR
WHEELHOUSE	DOORWAY

THOUGHTS & QUOTES

CONTENT WARNINGS	RATING

My Book Tracker

TITLE	AUTHOR
WHEELHOUSE	DOORWAY

THOUGHTS & QUOTES

CONTENT WARNINGS	RATING

My Book Tracker

TITLE	AUTHOR

WHEELHOUSE	DOORWAY

THOUGHTS & QUOTES

CONTENT WARNINGS	RATING

My Book Tracker

TITLE	AUTHOR
WHEELHOUSE	**DOORWAY**
THOUGHTS & QUOTES	
CONTENT WARNINGS	**RATING**

My Book Tracker

TITLE	**AUTHOR**
WHEELHOUSE	**DOORWAY**

THOUGHTS & QUOTES

CONTENT WARNINGS	**RATING**

My Book Tracker

TITLE	AUTHOR
WHEELHOUSE	DOORWAY
THOUGHTS & QUOTES	
CONTENT WARNINGS	RATING

My Book Tracker

TITLE	AUTHOR

WHEELHOUSE	DOORWAY

THOUGHTS & QUOTES

CONTENT WARNINGS	RATING

My Book Tracker

TITLE	AUTHOR
WHEELHOUSE	DOORWAY

THOUGHTS & QUOTES

CONTENT WARNINGS	RATING

My Book Tracker

TITLE	AUTHOR
WHEELHOUSE	**DOORWAY**
THOUGHTS & QUOTES	
CONTENT WARNINGS	**RATING**

My Book Tracker

TITLE	AUTHOR
WHEELHOUSE	**DOORWAY**

THOUGHTS & QUOTES

CONTENT WARNINGS	RATING

My Book Tracker

TITLE	AUTHOR
WHEELHOUSE	DOORWAY
THOUGHTS & QUOTES	
CONTENT WARNINGS	RATING

My Book Tracker

TITLE	AUTHOR
WHEELHOUSE	DOORWAY

THOUGHTS & QUOTES

CONTENT WARNINGS	RATING

My Book Tracker

TITLE	AUTHOR
WHEELHOUSE	**DOORWAY**
THOUGHTS & QUOTES	
CONTENT WARNINGS	**RATING**

My Book Tracker

TITLE	AUTHOR
WHEELHOUSE	DOORWAY

THOUGHTS & QUOTES

CONTENT WARNINGS	RATING

My Book Tracker

TITLE	AUTHOR
WHEELHOUSE	**DOORWAY**

THOUGHTS & QUOTES

CONTENT WARNINGS	RATING

My Book Tracker

TITLE	AUTHOR
WHEELHOUSE	DOORWAY

THOUGHTS & QUOTES

CONTENT WARNINGS	RATING

My Book Tracker

TITLE	AUTHOR

WHEELHOUSE	DOORWAY

THOUGHTS & QUOTES

CONTENT WARNINGS	RATING

My Book Tracker

TITLE	AUTHOR
WHEELHOUSE	**DOORWAY**

THOUGHTS & QUOTES

CONTENT WARNINGS	RATING

My Book Tracker

TITLE	AUTHOR
WHEELHOUSE	**DOORWAY**

THOUGHTS & QUOTES

CONTENT WARNINGS	RATING

My Book Tracker

TITLE	AUTHOR
WHEELHOUSE	**DOORWAY**
THOUGHTS & QUOTES	
CONTENT WARNINGS	**RATING**

My Book Tracker

TITLE	AUTHOR
WHEELHOUSE	DOORWAY

THOUGHTS & QUOTES

CONTENT WARNINGS	RATING

My Book Tracker

TITLE	AUTHOR
WHEELHOUSE	**DOORWAY**

THOUGHTS & QUOTES

CONTENT WARNINGS	RATING

My Book Tracker

TITLE	AUTHOR
WHEELHOUSE	DOORWAY

THOUGHTS & QUOTES

CONTENT WARNINGS	RATING

My Book Tracker

TITLE	AUTHOR
WHEELHOUSE	DOORWAY

THOUGHTS & QUOTES

CONTENT WARNINGS	RATING

My Book Tracker

TITLE	AUTHOR

WHEELHOUSE	DOORWAY

THOUGHTS & QUOTES

CONTENT WARNINGS	RATING

My Book Tracker

TITLE	**AUTHOR**
WHEELHOUSE	**DOORWAY**

THOUGHTS & QUOTES

CONTENT WARNINGS	**RATING**

My Book Tracker

TITLE	AUTHOR
WHEELHOUSE	DOORWAY
THOUGHTS & QUOTES	
CONTENT WARNINGS	RATING

My Book Tracker

TITLE	AUTHOR

WHEELHOUSE	DOORWAY

THOUGHTS & QUOTES

CONTENT WARNINGS	RATING

My Book Tracker

TITLE	AUTHOR
WHEELHOUSE	DOORWAY
THOUGHTS & QUOTES	
CONTENT WARNINGS	RATING

My Book Tracker

TITLE	**AUTHOR**
WHEELHOUSE	**DOORWAY**

THOUGHTS & QUOTES

CONTENT WARNINGS	**RATING**

My Book Tracker

TITLE	AUTHOR
WHEELHOUSE	DOORWAY

THOUGHTS & QUOTES

CONTENT WARNINGS	RATING

My Book Tracker

TITLE	AUTHOR
WHEELHOUSE	**DOORWAY**

THOUGHTS & QUOTES

CONTENT WARNINGS	RATING

My Book Tracker

TITLE	AUTHOR
WHEELHOUSE	DOORWAY
THOUGHTS & QUOTES	
CONTENT WARNINGS	RATING

My Book Tracker

TITLE	AUTHOR
WHEELHOUSE	DOORWAY

THOUGHTS & QUOTES

CONTENT WARNINGS	RATING

My Book Tracker

TITLE	AUTHOR

WHEELHOUSE	DOORWAY

THOUGHTS & QUOTES

CONTENT WARNINGS	RATING

My Book Tracker

TITLE	AUTHOR
WHEELHOUSE	DOORWAY
THOUGHTS & QUOTES	
CONTENT WARNINGS	RATING

My Book Tracker

TITLE	AUTHOR
WHEELHOUSE	DOORWAY

THOUGHTS & QUOTES

CONTENT WARNINGS	RATING

My Book Tracker

TITLE	AUTHOR

WHEELHOUSE	DOORWAY

THOUGHTS & QUOTES

CONTENT WARNINGS	RATING

My Book Tracker

TITLE	AUTHOR
WHEELHOUSE	DOORWAY

THOUGHTS & QUOTES

CONTENT WARNINGS	RATING

My Book Tracker

TITLE	AUTHOR

WHEELHOUSE	DOORWAY

THOUGHTS & QUOTES

CONTENT WARNINGS	RATING

My Book Tracker

TITLE	AUTHOR
WHEELHOUSE	DOORWAY

THOUGHTS & QUOTES

CONTENT WARNINGS	RATING

My Book Tracker

TITLE	AUTHOR

WHEELHOUSE	DOORWAY

THOUGHTS & QUOTES

CONTENT WARNINGS	RATING

My Book Tracker

TITLE	AUTHOR

WHEELHOUSE	DOORWAY

THOUGHTS & QUOTES

CONTENT WARNINGS	RATING

My Book Tracker

TITLE	AUTHOR
WHEELHOUSE	DOORWAY

THOUGHTS & QUOTES

CONTENT WARNINGS	RATING

My Book Tracker

TITLE	AUTHOR

WHEELHOUSE	DOORWAY

THOUGHTS & QUOTES

CONTENT WARNINGS	RATING

My Book Tracker

TITLE	AUTHOR
WHEELHOUSE	DOORWAY

THOUGHTS & QUOTES

CONTENT WARNINGS	RATING

My Book Tracker

TITLE	AUTHOR
WHEELHOUSE	DOORWAY
THOUGHTS & QUOTES	
CONTENT WARNINGS	RATING

My Book Tracker

TITLE	AUTHOR
WHEELHOUSE	**DOORWAY**

THOUGHTS & QUOTES

CONTENT WARNINGS	RATING

My Book Tracker

TITLE	**AUTHOR**
WHEELHOUSE	**DOORWAY**

THOUGHTS & QUOTES

CONTENT WARNINGS	**RATING**

My Book Tracker

TITLE	AUTHOR
WHEELHOUSE	DOORWAY

THOUGHTS & QUOTES

CONTENT WARNINGS	RATING

My Book Tracker

TITLE	AUTHOR
WHEELHOUSE	DOORWAY

THOUGHTS & QUOTES

CONTENT WARNINGS	RATING

My Book Tracker

TITLE	AUTHOR

WHEELHOUSE	DOORWAY

THOUGHTS & QUOTES

CONTENT WARNINGS	RATING

My Book Tracker

TITLE	AUTHOR
WHEELHOUSE	DOORWAY

THOUGHTS & QUOTES

CONTENT WARNINGS	RATING

My Book Tracker

TITLE	AUTHOR
WHEELHOUSE	DOORWAY

THOUGHTS & QUOTES

CONTENT WARNINGS	RATING

My Book Tracker

TITLE	AUTHOR
WHEELHOUSE	DOORWAY

THOUGHTS & QUOTES

CONTENT WARNINGS	RATING

My Book Tracker

TITLE	AUTHOR

WHEELHOUSE	DOORWAY

THOUGHTS & QUOTES

CONTENT WARNINGS	RATING

My Book Tracker

TITLE	AUTHOR
WHEELHOUSE	DOORWAY

THOUGHTS & QUOTES

CONTENT WARNINGS	RATING

My Book Tracker

TITLE	AUTHOR
WHEELHOUSE	**DOORWAY**
THOUGHTS & QUOTES	
CONTENT WARNINGS	**RATING**

My Book Tracker

TITLE	AUTHOR

WHEELHOUSE	DOORWAY

THOUGHTS & QUOTES

CONTENT WARNINGS	RATING

My Book Tracker

TITLE	AUTHOR
WHEELHOUSE	DOORWAY

THOUGHTS & QUOTES

CONTENT WARNINGS	RATING

My Book Tracker

TITLE	AUTHOR
WHEELHOUSE	DOORWAY
THOUGHTS & QUOTES	
CONTENT WARNINGS	RATING

My Book Tracker

TITLE	AUTHOR
WHEELHOUSE	DOORWAY

THOUGHTS & QUOTES

CONTENT WARNINGS	RATING

My Book Tracker

TITLE	AUTHOR

WHEELHOUSE	DOORWAY

THOUGHTS & QUOTES

CONTENT WARNINGS	RATING

My Book Tracker

TITLE	AUTHOR
WHEELHOUSE	DOORWAY

THOUGHTS & QUOTES

CONTENT WARNINGS	RATING

My Book Tracker

TITLE	AUTHOR
WHEELHOUSE	DOORWAY

THOUGHTS & QUOTES

CONTENT WARNINGS	RATING

My Book Tracker

TITLE	AUTHOR
WHEELHOUSE	DOORWAY
THOUGHTS & QUOTES	
CONTENT WARNINGS	RATING

My Book Tracker

TITLE	AUTHOR

WHEELHOUSE	DOORWAY

THOUGHTS & QUOTES

CONTENT WARNINGS	RATING

My Book Tracker

TITLE	AUTHOR
WHEELHOUSE	DOORWAY

THOUGHTS & QUOTES

CONTENT WARNINGS	RATING

My Book Tracker

TITLE	AUTHOR
WHEELHOUSE	DOORWAY

THOUGHTS & QUOTES

CONTENT WARNINGS	RATING

My Book Tracker

TITLE	AUTHOR
WHEELHOUSE	**DOORWAY**

THOUGHTS & QUOTES

CONTENT WARNINGS	RATING

My Book Tracker

TITLE	AUTHOR
WHEELHOUSE	DOORWAY

THOUGHTS & QUOTES

CONTENT WARNINGS	RATING

My Book Tracker

TITLE	AUTHOR
WHEELHOUSE	DOORWAY

THOUGHTS & QUOTES

CONTENT WARNINGS	RATING

My Book Tracker

TITLE	AUTHOR
WHEELHOUSE	DOORWAY

THOUGHTS & QUOTES

CONTENT WARNINGS	RATING

My Book Tracker

TITLE	AUTHOR

WHEELHOUSE	DOORWAY

THOUGHTS & QUOTES

CONTENT WARNINGS	RATING

My Book Tracker

TITLE	AUTHOR
WHEELHOUSE	DOORWAY

THOUGHTS & QUOTES

CONTENT WARNINGS	RATING

My Book Tracker

TITLE	AUTHOR

WHEELHOUSE	DOORWAY

THOUGHTS & QUOTES

CONTENT WARNINGS	RATING

My Book Tracker

TITLE	AUTHOR

WHEELHOUSE	DOORWAY

THOUGHTS & QUOTES

CONTENT WARNINGS	RATING

My Book Tracker

TITLE	AUTHOR
WHEELHOUSE	DOORWAY

THOUGHTS & QUOTES

CONTENT WARNINGS	RATING

My Book Tracker

TITLE	AUTHOR
WHEELHOUSE	DOORWAY

THOUGHTS & QUOTES

CONTENT WARNINGS	RATING

My Book Tracker

TITLE	AUTHOR
WHEELHOUSE	DOORWAY

THOUGHTS & QUOTES

CONTENT WARNINGS	RATING

My Book Tracker

TITLE	AUTHOR
WHEELHOUSE	DOORWAY

THOUGHTS & QUOTES

CONTENT WARNINGS	RATING

My Book Tracker

TITLE	AUTHOR
WHEELHOUSE	DOORWAY
THOUGHTS & QUOTES	
CONTENT WARNINGS	RATING

My Book Tracker

TITLE	**AUTHOR**
WHEELHOUSE	**DOORWAY**

THOUGHTS & QUOTES

CONTENT WARNINGS	**RATING**

My Book Tracker

TITLE	AUTHOR
WHEELHOUSE	DOORWAY

THOUGHTS & QUOTES

CONTENT WARNINGS	RATING

My Book Tracker

TITLE	AUTHOR
WHEELHOUSE	DOORWAY
THOUGHTS & QUOTES	
CONTENT WARNINGS	RATING

My Book Tracker

TITLE	AUTHOR
WHEELHOUSE	DOORWAY

THOUGHTS & QUOTES

CONTENT WARNINGS	RATING

My Book Tracker

TITLE	**AUTHOR**
WHEELHOUSE	**DOORWAY**
THOUGHTS & QUOTES	
CONTENT WARNINGS	**RATING**

My Book Tracker

TITLE	AUTHOR
WHEELHOUSE	DOORWAY

THOUGHTS & QUOTES

CONTENT WARNINGS	RATING

My Book Tracker

TITLE	AUTHOR
WHEELHOUSE	DOORWAY

THOUGHTS & QUOTES

CONTENT WARNINGS	RATING

My Book Tracker

TITLE	AUTHOR
WHEELHOUSE	DOORWAY

THOUGHTS & QUOTES

CONTENT WARNINGS	RATING

My Book Tracker

TITLE	AUTHOR
WHEELHOUSE	DOORWAY

THOUGHTS & QUOTES

CONTENT WARNINGS	RATING

My Book Tracker

TITLE	AUTHOR
WHEELHOUSE	DOORWAY

THOUGHTS & QUOTES

CONTENT WARNINGS	RATING

My Book Tracker

TITLE	AUTHOR

WHEELHOUSE	DOORWAY

THOUGHTS & QUOTES

CONTENT WARNINGS	RATING

My Book Tracker

TITLE	AUTHOR
WHEELHOUSE	DOORWAY

THOUGHTS & QUOTES

CONTENT WARNINGS	RATING

My Book Tracker

TITLE	AUTHOR
WHEELHOUSE	DOORWAY

THOUGHTS & QUOTES

CONTENT WARNINGS	RATING

My Book Tracker

TITLE	AUTHOR

WHEELHOUSE	DOORWAY

THOUGHTS & QUOTES

CONTENT WARNINGS	RATING

My Book Tracker

TITLE	AUTHOR

WHEELHOUSE	DOORWAY

THOUGHTS & QUOTES

CONTENT WARNINGS	RATING

My Book Tracker

TITLE	AUTHOR
WHEELHOUSE	**DOORWAY**
THOUGHTS & QUOTES	
CONTENT WARNINGS	**RATING**

Additional Notes

Additional Notes

Additional Notes

Additional Notes

Additional Notes

Additional Notes

Additional Notes

Additional Notes

Additional Notes

Additional Notes

Glossary

Backlist: books that have been published for at least a year

Blurb: a short, positive endorsement on a book's jacket from a publication or another author

Book hangover: the feeling you get after you've read a book that was so great that it feels like no other can compare

Book slump: when you just don't feel like reading

BookTok and Bookstagram: the bookish communities on TikTok and Instagram, respectively

Buzzy: when a book is popular, critically acclaimed, or widely discussed in the bookish community

DNF: did not finish

Doghouse: the group of subjects, tropes, themes, etc., that turn you off from reading or finishing a book

Dump: to stop reading a book

Epistolary: a novel told in the form of letters (also emails or texts)

Frontlist: books that have been released within the last year, also known as new releases

Handselling: when a bookseller recommends a book

Honker: a huge book, usually over 500 pages

POV: point of view

Retelling: a book that takes an existing story, such as a fairy tale or a piece of classic literature, and recasts it in a new form

Sunken page fallacy: when you've read enough of a book that you don't want to dump it because you've already put in a lot of time

TBR: to be read

Trope: a common theme or literary device

Unreliable narrator: when the credibility of the narrator cannot be trusted

Wheelhouse: the group of subjects, tropes, themes, etc., that make you want to read a book

weldon**owen**

an imprint of Insight Editions

P.O. Box 3088
San Rafael, CA 94912
www.weldonowen.com

CEO Raoul Goff
VP Publisher Roger Shaw
Editorial Director Katie Killebrew
Editor Kayla Belser
VP, Creative Director Chrissy Kwasnik
Art Director Ashley Quackenbush
Senior Designer Stephanie Odeh
VP Manufacturing Alix Nicholaeff
Production Associate Tiffani Patterson
Sr Production Manager, Subsidiary Rights Lina s Palma-Temena

Weldon Owen would also like to thank Karen Levy for copyediting and Bob Cooper for proofreading.

Illustrations by Rebecca Santo

ISBN: 979-8-88674-194-0

Manufactured in China by Insight Editions
10 9 8 7 6 5 4 3

maybe
later

maybe later
maybe later